Original title:
Life: A Riddle Wrapped in a Conundrum

Copyright © 2025 Creative Arts Management OÜ
All rights reserved.

Author: George Mercer
ISBN HARDBACK: 978-1-80566-216-7
ISBN PAPERBACK: 978-1-80566-511-3

The Secrets We Breathe

Whispers of secrets hide in our breath,
Tickling the minds, teasing the depths.
With laughter we dance, and joy we weave,
In the chaos of thoughts, we learn to believe.

The mustard on bacon, the socks that don't pair,
Are hints of a puzzle, beyond compare.
When logic goes plaid and reason takes flight,
We giggle and ponder till day turns to night.

Vignettes of the Unknown

A cat steals my sandwich, a pig wears a hat,
A frog claims a throne, on the mat he sat.
In snippets of odd, confusion abounds,
With onions and laughter, our joy knows no bounds.

Cards shaped like pickles, and clocks run away,
What time is it anyway? Just a game to play.
As truth juggles whimsy in moments gone past,
We scribble our thoughts, hoping they'll last.

Tangled in Reality

The spaghetti is twirling, it whispers my name,
A wall clock is laughing, I'm losing the game.
With socks on my hands, I attempt to write,
This riddle of odd—a comical sight!

Mirror, mirror, on the wall, what's true?
Today I'm a unicorn wrapped in blue goo.
As jellybeans tumble from pockets we share,
We gather the pieces, peculiar yet fair.

The Journey of Illusions

A monkey on bikes shows me the way,
To dodge the absurdities that brighten the day.
With pancakes like planets and syrupy stars,
We sail on the tides of our giggles and jars.

So grab hold of nonsense and dance through the rain,
Splash puddles of laughter, ignore any pain.
In this enchanting riddle we'll forever find,
The answers we seek—just a tease of the mind.

A Tapestry of Questions

In a world of swirling thoughts,
Where answers hide like shy young tots,
We chase the clues, we scratch our heads,
While socks go missing from our beds.

Why do we trip on our own feet?
Is coffee stronger than a cheat?
With every sip, we ponder more,
And question why we snooze and snore.

A duck in pants and hat so grand,
Claims all the wisdom that he planned.
With wobbly wisdom, he takes flight,
Making sense in the dead of night.

So twist and twirl in this grand jest,
Enjoy the chaos, and join the quest.
For in the jokes that tickle the brain,
The answers hide, but there's much to gain.

The Light Behind the Curtain

Behind the curtain, shadows dance,
With riddles that invite a glance.
A talking cat strums on a lyre,
While socks and sandals start a choir.

Why does the chicken cross the street?
To see if the grass tastes like a treat?
With every peck, a giggle pops,
As clowns on unicycles bust some hops.

A goldfish wearing polka dots,
Claims he knows all the paradox.
He swims in circles, thinks it wise,
While plotting schemes to eat the flies.

When answers come in bursts of glee,
We laugh and spin just like a bee.
So hold on tight to whimsy's reign,
And let the laughter break the chain.

Unfolding the Enigma

A cat in a hat sings a tune,
While dancing with spoons under the moon.
Questions come spinning in circles,
Like squirrels who gossip in sparkly hurdles.

Jellybeans whisper with joyful delight,
Telling secrets that tickle the night.
Mysteries wrapped in a brightly colored bow,
Where do socks vanish? No one seems to know!

The Hidden Meaning of Moments

A sandwich says, 'I'm not just a snack!'
With secrets of pickles and mustard stacked.
In every small bite, there's a tale to unfold,
Of journeys through toasters, both brave and bold.

Chickens cross roads with a wink and a nod,
Seeking answers, perhaps finding God.
In a world of puns, where laughter ignites,
Even the marshmallows float to new heights!

Clocks That Ticktock in Silence

Ticking like secrets beneath the bed,
A clock made of jelly, too wobbly to tread.
Hands spinning wildly, lost in the fuss,
Counting the giggles in a raucous bus.

Time slips away on banana peels,
Where every second is spinning with feels.
What did yesterday's breakfast really say?
It's hidden in pancakes that dance on a tray!

Beneath the Mask of the Ordinary

A potato dons glasses, reads the news,
While an onion ponders why it snooze.
Every toaster's a wizard with marvelous spells,
Cooking up magic, ringing joyful bells.

In the kaleidoscope of the day-to-day,
Fries dream of freedom, and beans long to play.
Beneath each odd surface, a surprise awaits,
With laughter and wonder opening the gates!

Chasing the Unseen

I chased a shadow across the street,
It smiled at me with mischievous glee.
I asked it what made it so fleet,
It whispered secrets, then dashed off with a plea.

Are we the chasers or the chased,
In this game where time runs free?
I tripped on thoughts, a bit misplaced,
And laughed with the breeze, oh, how carefree!

Every corner hides a clue,
Yet I forgot where I left my shoes.
The invisible yarn, tight and askew,
Unraveling mysteries, oh what a ruse!

In pursuit of the unseen prize,
I realized I'm just a passing ghost.
Chasing shadows under bright blue skies,
And in that chase, I find my joy the most.

A Simmering Pot of Paradoxes

In a pot where thoughts bubble and churn,
I tossed in dreams and a dash of doubt.
The lid won't close, so I watch and learn,
As logic dances, trying to pout.

Stirring up chaos, a pinch of fun,
Who knows what flavors will emerge?
Sometimes I laugh, sometimes I run,
As sprinkle of sense begins to verge.

Each thought a noodle, tangled and bright,
Some twirl like ballerinas, others fall flat.
Yet every morsel hints at delight,
In this simmering pot, I chat with my cat.

So here's a spoonful, take a taste,
Not every recipe needs a guide.
In this paradox, there's no haste,
Just stir and enjoy the crazy ride.

The Fabric of What Could Be

With threads of wishes, I weave my day,
Stitching joy through the seams of dread.
Every block I build, a quirky display,
With laughter echoing, it's finely spread.

I cut out patterns of dreams gone wrong,
And use them as patches, bright and bold.
Though sometimes it feels like a meaningless song,
I wear the fabric, letting tales unfold.

The needle pokes at a truth or two,
While colors clash in a dance divine.
I can't decide if the skies are blue,
Or if these crazy shades waltz on a line.

With each snip, I create my art,
A tapestry messy, yet full of flair.
In the chaos, I find a quirky heart,
Stitching together what's really rare.

Stories in Flux

Once upon a time, or so they say,
The clock ticked backward, ticks turned to tacks.
A dragon read books on a rainy day,
While knights slid on socks, avoiding the cracks.

In stories where logic ties its shoe,
Every plot twists like a pretzel in knits.
Heroes lose crowns but don't have a clue,
As villains tell jokes and share silly skits.

Pages flip like birds on the wing,
Feathers of hopes toss in a breeze.
Every narrative wants to sing,
But some just get lost in quirky unease.

However we read them, they bend and sway,
In the theater of cosmic giggles wide.
So join in the antics, let's all play,
Our stories will flow like a crazy tide.

The Tapestry of Existence

Threads weave and twine, quite absurd,
Each stitch is a question, sometimes unheard.
Patterns grow wild, like a cat on a chair,
Laughter erupts, tangled thoughts everywhere.

Colors collide, a patchwork of grace,
Stumbling through moments, we trip through the space.
Knots to unravel, and some to enjoy,
In this crazy quilt, we find our own joy.

Life flips and flops, like a fish out of stream,
Chasing the bizarre, like it's all just a dream.
Caffeine and chaos, the fabric unfolds,
We'll dance through the mayhem, be brave and be bold.

Questions in the Breeze

Whispers of thoughts float up to the sky,
Like kites in the wind, they swirl and they fly.
Why do we ponder, why do we guess?
Perhaps we're just jesters, dressing in mess.

Curiosity tickles, the heart gives a poke,
We giggle at mysteries, tangled in smoke.
Do ducks have dreams? Do clouds ever sigh?
In questioning laughter, let giggles comply.

The breeze carries secrets, a riddle or two,
Twirling around as they say, "What's true?"
In folly we stumble, with each passing gust,
Questions are tasty, laugh turns to dust.

Labyrinthine Journeys

Wandering paths where the lost find their feet,
Step left or step right, it's a dance, oh so sweet.
Traps made of logic, yet laughter's the prize,
We skip through the maze, where confusions arise.

The walls start to giggle, as we walk on by,
Pretzels of thought, swirling up to the sky.
Who said it was easy? Don't ask the old sage,
The map's upside down, let's laugh at this stage.

Turn back or go forward, we flip like a coin,
Choices like jellybeans, all we do is join.
In this wacky puzzle, we find joy in the bend,
A twist and a shout, what a merry weekend!

The Dance of Paradoxes

Footsteps in rhythm, a twist and a turn,
We dance life's conundrums, and laughter we learn.
A hop and a skip, then a slide to the side,
In this topsy-turvy, joy's our true guide.

Silly and solemn, we whirl like a breeze,
Explaining the unexplainable with ease.
Is it hot? Is it cold? The world spins around,
In quirky confusion, our happiness found.

Twists that bewilder, as reason takes flight,
In the humor of chaos, everything's right.
Laughing through puzzles, we twirl and we sway,
In the joyous absurdity, we find our way.

Navigating the Unknown

In a world that's full of maze,
We dance through folly, sing in haze.
With maps that lead to nowhere fast,
We stumble, trip, but have a blast.

Each path we take a game of chance,
A crazy waltz, an awkward dance.
With questions missing all the clues,
We laugh in shades of vibrant blues.

The Conundrum of Choices

Too many doors, too few keyholes,
Flip a coin, here come the trolls.
Do I pick this, or do I that?
Is it a choice, or just a spat?

Each decision comes with a twist,
Like a circus act, it can't be missed.
With options piling to the sky,
I choose to just bake a pie.

Surfaces and Depths

Like onions layered, we peel away,
What's inside? Just kids at play.
We wear our smiles and silly hats,
But roll and tumble with the cats.

The truth is brisk, but humor's strong,
We dance with shadows all night long.
In crazy depths, we find the light,
And laugh about it every night.

Clockwork of the Heart

Tick-tock goes the silly clock,
It winds around like a cheeky sock.
With love's gears clanging out of tune,
We pirouette under a lopsided moon.

Each heartbeat whispers jokes and jives,
In this merry dance, everyone thrives.
With every tick ensuring fun,
We laugh, we love, until we're done.

Questions in the Wind

Why do shoes always go astray?
I swear they plot their getaway.
Do socks have secret lives at night?
A mystery wrapped in cotton tight.

If cats could speak, what would they say?
"Feed me tuna, then go away!"
Do goldfish dream of ocean blue?
Or just swim circles, who really knew?

Is ice cream the answer to every woe?
As long as it melts nice and slow.
Do mirrors reflect our greatest fears?
Or just our hair and aging years?

Questions flutter, dance, and spin,
In this world, where do we begin?
Each query swirling like a kite,
In the breeze of day and night.

The Unsought Answers

Why do we trip over our own feet?
Do we walk on eggshells on the street?
If thoughts could talk, what would they shout?
Would they cheer us on or cause a rout?

Do elephants really forget our names?
While we remember all their silly games?
Is cereal soup in a bowl so deep?
Questions that haunt us in our sleep.

What if clouds are just cotton candy?
And rain is lemonade, oh so dandy?
Do fishes know they swim in blue?
Or are they blissful, with no clue?

Unsought answers float and glide,
Like lost balloons we cannot hide.
The more we ponder, the less we find,
This funny riddle we call the mind.

Whirlpools of Thought

Why do we worry about silly things?
Like how much joy a bad haircut brings?
Do shoes with laces tie themselves tight?
Or do they plot their escape at night?

In whirlpools of thought, we spin and twirl,
Searching for gems in a chaotic whirl.
Do clocks really care if we're late for work?
Or do they giggle like some sly jerk?

Why does the fridge hum a sweet tune?
While leftovers dance like a ghostly boon?
If bread could talk, would it have a plan?
To toast our mornings, or just be bland?

In swirling thoughts where giggles collide,
We laugh at riddles that never subside.
Chasing the waves of quirky clues,
In this sea of questions, we often lose.

The Tapestry of Questions

What stitches questions in our minds?
Is it the coffee or the things it binds?
Do plants gossip when we're not near?
Sharing secrets they can't make clear?

Why do we laugh at all the wrong times?
Like at someone's slip, in silly rhymes?
Is life just a game of peek-a-boo?
With all the questions that we pursue?

If shadows had thoughts, what would they say?
"We're just here, waiting for the day!"
Are dreams merely puzzles we can't solve?
Or a tapestry of quirks that evolve?

Interwoven threads of what and why,
Forms a funny quilt that flutters high.
Each question a knot, each answer a thread,
In this tapestry of jest, we tread.

Threads That Bind Us

In a world of tangled string,
We laugh at what we bring.
Knots that twist our minds so tight,
Yet we dance, embracing the light.

Stitch by stitch, we sew our fate,
Wobbly paths that make us wait.
With every pull and every tug,
We find our joy, a cozy hug.

Beyond the Walls of Knowing

Peeking over fences high,
Wondering just how to fly.
Secrets scribbled in the air,
Oh, the trouble we all bear!

With binoculars of doubt and fear,
We spy on dreams that disappear.
Yet in the chaos, there we stand,
Painting murals with a hand.

The Hidden Currents of Existence

Life's a river, swift and sly,
Flowing here and asking why.
With rubber ducks and silly hats,
We paddle through, avoiding spats.

Currents pull from every side,
But in the waves, we choose to ride.
Splashing laughter, wild and free,
Unraveling the mystery.

The Echo of Forgotten Pathways

Echoes bounce down dusty roads,
Where laughter lightens heavy loads.
We wander paths both old and new,
In shoes too big, or perhaps just two.

Each step a puzzle piece we chase,
With twirling doubts and endless grace.
In every stumble, we embrace,
The silly dance of time and space.

Layers of Thoughts Unfolding

In the garden where ideas bloom,
A jester dances, dispelling gloom.
With each layer peeled, we laugh and sigh,
Questions tumble like apples from the sky.

What's the riddle behind a sneeze?
Is it just pollen or universal tease?
Wrapped in thoughts like a burrito tight,
We munch on mysteries, day and night.

The Enigma of Everyday

Why did the chicken cross the road,
To solve a riddle or just to bode?
Daily puzzles fly near and far,
Like a lost sock that's caught in a car.

Coffee spills like feelings unmet,
Every sip comes with a new bet.
Is it caffeine or the dawn's bright tune?
We laugh at the chaos, morning's cartoon.

Journals of the Unconscious

In dreams, I scribble my witty thoughts,
Unraveling truths and silly knots.
A sock with stripes, a cat in a hat,
Who knew my brain would chat like that?

I pen my fears in color so bright,
Monsters dance in the pale moonlight.
What's the secret behind the snore?
Maybe it's wisdom knocking at the door.

A Quest Among Shadows

In shadows deep where giggles echo,
I seek the answers from both high and low.
A flashlight flickers, becomes a star,
I chase shiny truths, what a bizarre bazaar!

Do shadows hold secrets or just lost shoes?
Perhaps they're hiding from the day's abuse.
With each step, I trip over my thought,
A comedic ballet—who knew I'd have fought?

Echoes in a Labyrinth

In a maze where whispers play,
Lost socks debate, 'Where's my mate?'
Clocks tick backward, what a show,
Time winks at us, 'Just go slow!'

Rabbits wear hats, it's quite bizarre,
Chasing dreams in a candy car.
A cat plays chess, hisses with flair,
Says, 'Take a seat, don't you dare stare!'

Mirrors reflect more than just dread,
They giggle and wink at what's ahead.
Questions bounce like rubber balls,
Duck down quick, or risk the falls!

Jumbled thoughts in a paper hat,
Spinning circles like a dizzy cat.
Round and round, let's have a laugh,
In this maze, we find our path!

Secrets Beneath the Surface

Underneath the sturdy ground,
Gnomes hold secrets, quite profound.
They brew tea with worms and sigh,
'Why'd the chicken even try?'

Stars gossip from their velvet beds,
Raccoons juggle, balancing threads.
Who stole the moon? Oh, such a crime!
She was just out to see the thyme!

A fish thinks that it's quite a bird,
Flapping fins while feeling absurd.
Turtles dance with shoes that squeak,
While daisies giggle, 'You're a freak!'

Worms in top hats plot their scheme,
To take over the world, it's their dream.
Yet, as they plot, we sway in grass,
Laughing at secrets, time will pass!

Enigma of the Heart

In a jar, feelings spin and twirl,
Emotions dance, a dizzy whirl.
Hearts have jackets, colorful and bright,
Whispers of love, oh what a sight!

A pineapple sings a tune so sweet,
While dancing shoes skip to the beat.
Chocolate dreams melt in the sun,
Twisted tales where all have fun!

Jumbled puzzles fit with laughs,
Finding joy in silly drafts.
Love in socks, mismatched as art,
A quirky riddle, the enigma of the heart!

Balloons float high, ready to burst,
Filled with giggles, an airy thirst.
In this bloom of chaos so neat,
We find our joy, oh what a treat!

Shadows of Tomorrow

Tomorrow's shadows, twist and sway,
Chasing things that went astray.
Chickens cluck in philosophical trends,
Debating if we're all just friends!

Clouds wear pajamas, oh what a sight,
They snore loudly through the night.
Stars sneak peeks from under their sheets,
Throwing wishes like tasty treats.

A snail on a skateboard, speedy and spry,
Whispers to crickets, 'Oh me, oh my!'
What's around the corner, who can say?
Just skate through the shadows, laugh all the way!

Twisting paths lead to roads unknown,
Yet laughter bubbles like a cheerful tone.
In the twilight, we find our cheer,
Embracing the mystery, year after year!

A Journey Without an End

I packed my bags with socks and dreams,
But it's the chases that burst at the seams.
I asked the map for a way to go,
It winked at me, said "Bro, just flow."

The road ahead's a twisty game,
One foot in mud, the other in fame.
My GPS laughed, took a wild turn,
Now I'm here, just craving to learn.

I met a cow who said "Moo!"
I asked for wisdom, but got a stew.
The travels seem endless, oh what a fright,
But the snacks on the way bring such delight!

So here I am with a grin so wide,
Collecting the moments, my goofy pride.
Each step I take, a waddle of glee,
For what's a journey, if not a spree?

Secrets in Ordinary Things

The toaster's secret, it speaks in toast,
Burnt edges shout, "I matter most!"
Coffee cups hold meetings, I swear,
Discussing how not one mug should share.

The fridge hums tunes of midnight snacks,
While leftovers plot their daring attacks.
A spoon dreams of dancing, embracing a bowl,
Pasta does twirls, it's a carb-fueled goal.

Dust bunnies mock me, they're running a show,
In the corners they gather, just to say "Hello!"
The remote hides well, thinks it's so sly,
Yet on the couch, I hear it cry.

Every mundane moment, a treasure to find,
Wrapped in the chaos, a joy intertwined.
For within the small things, secrets do sing,
And laughter spills out as I dance with my king.

The Veil of Possibility

I woke up today wrapped in a dream,
With breakfast choices that gleam and scream.
Eggs dance lightly on a sizzling pan,
While toast joins in, like a jolly band.

The sun plays peekaboo, what a tease,
"Am I too bright?" it asks with ease.
Clouds are hitchhikers, floating up high,
Whispering secrets as they flutter by.

There's magic in traffic, a honking song,
Every red light a reminder of wrong.
Yet in this chaos, I laugh with glee,
As I race with squirrels who cling to a tree.

So here's to the chance, the flip of a fate,
Each step a riddle, each pause, first-rate.
In this curtain of what-ifs, wild and free,
I find joy's laughter – it's living with glee!

Cascades of Unanswered Questions

Why do socks vanish? Where do they flee?
Maybe they dance with the dust bunnies, you see.
Questions like bubbles, they pop and they burst,
Leaving me laughing, oh isn't that cursed?

Can a cat open doors, or is it just me?
Each pounce a riddle; it's far from easy.
"Are you even listening?" I ask my old chair,
It creaks in tune, like it doesn't care.

Why is the clock always ticking so fast?
Time's sneaky fox, it's here then it's past.
The fridge hums nonsense, a witty old sage,
Offering laughter at this curious age.

So cheers to the queries that dance in the mind,
In this riddle of life, laughter's the find.
For though answers elude, like a cat with a yarn,
I'll chuckle through questions, and share this sweet charm.

The Color of Uncertainty

In a world of shades and hues,
We dance on the rainbow's clues.
Purple like the grapes of doubt,
Orange when your hopes scream out.

The paint smudged on the canvas bright,
Stripes of joy, yet fears take flight.
Every color's a wild guess,
Splashing truth in a fancy dress.

Each brushstroke laughs in our face,
Tickling thoughts at a bustling pace.
A palette where the colors blend,
Guessing what the next trend will send.

So grab your brush and toss the paint,
Embrace the chaos; there's no complaint.
For uncertainty is quite the show,
Where colors shift and giggles flow.

Reflections in a Broken Mirror

In shards of glass we see our grins,
A hundred faces, where to begin?
The jokes we tell in fragmented light,
Who's the clown in this broken sight?

Reflections warp like a funhouse ride,
Laughter echoes, we run, we hide.
Each piece shows a different pose,
Am I the hero? Or just a nose?

The more I try to fix the glass,
The greater the giggles as we pass.
Every fracture tells a story told,
In smoothest gloss, our truths unfold.

Jump through the gaps, and you may find,
A chuckle echoing in your mind.
What's real or not? A jester's dance,
In broken mirrors, we take our chance.

Puzzles of Solitude

In solitude, I juggle thoughts,
Like puzzle pieces, oh so fraught.
A corner here, the edge not fit,
Solving mysteries, just a bit.

The cat's my coach, she watches me,
As I put together what's not to see.
Each misplaced piece, a laugh we share,
My isolation's a funny affair.

I whisper to the missing parts,
"Come join the fun, don't break my heart!"
But they hide away in their own game,
Leaving me with puzzles to tame.

So here I sit with a cheeky grin,
In the quiet, where giggles begin.
The riddles dance in shadows twirled,
Solitude? A joyfully silly world.

Whispers Between the Lines

Between the lines, where secrets play,
Whispers of jest lead us astray.
A chuckle here, a wink gone wrong,
In the margins, we all belong.

The stories loop like spaghetti threads,
Twisting thoughts in our crowded heads.
Each little inkblot leaves its trace,
A doodle forming a funny face.

As we read on, the text may shift,
Words giggle and tease, a comical gift.
Poems can tickle, make you ponder,
A riddle you seek, a thought to wander.

So flip the page, let laughter grow,
In whispers hidden, let giggles flow.
For between the lines, we find the jest,
Life's little quirks, a playful quest.

The Poetry of Paradox

A cat that barks, a dog that meows,
The mayor's in pajamas, what a sight to arouse!
Time melts like ice on a summer day,
Just don't ask the clocks, they've all gone astray.

The fish take flight, while the birds dive deep,
In dreams of flying, the penguins leap!
Upside down is really the right way around,
Who knew such mischief could always astound?

The sun sets in morning, while morning is night,
Chaos and order are just soft and bright!
Words of wisdom in riddles they hide,
Chasing our tails, we'll go for a ride.

So strap on your shoes, let's waltz with the weird,
Join the odd parade, where laughter is cheered!
The rhythm of riddles gives us quite the thrill,
In this dance of confusion, we find our own skill.

Mosaic of Yesterday, Today, Tomorrow

Yesterday's dreams are today's silly jokes,
Tomorrow is wearing yesterday's coats.
When the sun greets the moon in a silly duet,
It's the giggles of time, and we're not done yet.

The future asks questions that haunt the past,
Like a turtle in fast-forward, it's moving too fast.
We flip through our calendars, seeking the clues,
Yet calendars whisper, 'You'll snooze what you choose!'

Moments like crayons, all colored and bright,
Each stroke a reminder, to laugh in the light.
Yesterday's greens, with today's hues of blue,
A mosaic of moments, a puzzling view.

Right now's just a waiting room, tickets all torn,
Sipping on sunshine, bathed in the scorn.
If time is a jigsaw, we'll piece it with glee,
Tomorrow's a puzzle we're yet to see!

Fables of the Forgotten

The turtle that danced with a slippered shoe,
Told tales to the frogs, who all disagreed too!
A dragon that sneezed, turned cities to dust,
In the fables of folly, we place our trust.

Once a snail raced with a lightning bug,
The finish line shattered, the world gave a shrug.
The hare was confused, as he lost track of time,
In a race against logic, what's jumbled is prime!

We speak of lost wisdom as grandpas will do,
But their tales are tipsy, all muddled and blue.
Fables tell secrets that twist and kaboom,
Each laugh is a riddle, a song in the room.

So gather the stories that tickle your brain,
In echoes of laughter, we'll never feel pain.
For in every misstep, a lesson we find,
In the fables of jest, we leave worries behind.

Chasing Shadows of Truth

The truth is a squirrel that hides in a tree,
Dances and dodges, giggling with glee.
Each shadow it casts seems to tell a new tale,
But it swims like a fish when we're setting a sail.

A riddle approaches, wearing polka-dot shoes,
Asks why the chicken has something to lose.
It flaps in the wind, a joker in disguise,
What's dark may be light, to smarten the flies.

The reflection in puddles plays tricks on the eye,
A whispered adventure, so witty, oh my!
We run after shadows, with nets made of dreams,
In a world of confusion, or so it seems.

So join in the chase, where nothing is clear,
With whimsy we frolic, not losing a cheer.
For in every pursuit of the curious night,
We discover such truths that ignite pure delight.

Journey Through the Fog

In a foggy lane, I wander slow,
Questions dance, and answers grow.
Socks to shoes, are they a pair?
Maybe it's just my wild hair!

Coffee spills, jokes in the air,
Lost my keys, but who's to care?
A squirrel's cheek is full of nuts,
Is it laughter, or just my guts?

I trip on thoughts, I slip on dreams,
Reality tears at the seams.
Chasing shadows, what a hoot,
Wobbly minds in silly pursuit!

Through the mist, a grin unfolds,
More questions than I ever told.
With each step, I find the jest,
In muddled paths, I feel the best!

The Riddle of Our Echoes.

In a room, loud echoes sing,
Muffled words of springtime fling.
Who said that? Is it really true?
Can a whisper weigh like a shoe?

Chasing echoes of last week's fun,
Was it you, or the clever sun?
Laughter clinks like glasses raised,
Are we lost, or merely amazed?

Amidst the noise, truth plays hide and seek,
Finding it might take a cheeky peak.
"Knock-knock," who's there with a grin?
Is it wisdom, or just a twin?

Each chuckle bounces, zigzags wide,
Reflecting thoughts we sometimes hide.
In echoes, there's a silly chance,
To laugh at what makes us dance!

Whispers of the Unseen

In shadows soft, whispers start,
Tales of mischief, a cheeky heart.
Pets that plan a midnight feast,
Or socks that vanish, at least!

A breeze carries giggles near,
What's that noise? Just the cat, I fear!
A riddle wrapped in cotton fluff,
Who knew silence could be so tough?

Behind closed doors, secrets leap,
Tick-Tock clocks make faces steep.
Do walls laugh, or do they sigh?
Invisible jesters, oh my, oh my!

In unseen realms, mischief plays,
What a crazy, curious maze!
Every whisper holds a tease,
In the silence, we find our breeze!

The Puzzle of our Days

Jigsaw pieces on the floor,
Did we start, or end up more?
Coffee cups and timers race,
Riddles hide in every space.

What's for breakfast? It's a game,
Oatmeal's fine, but what's its name?
Is today, also just a dream?
Or are we all a winning team?

With quirky friends, the world's our joke,
Each pun pricks like a friendly poke.
Through fumbles, we shape our way,
Finding joy in each odd day!

At this puzzle, let's all stare,
Isn't fun beyond compare?
In these moments, laughter stays,
As we dance through all our days!

The Veil of Questions

What's this strange game we all play?
With punchlines hidden in the fray.
Is it jokes or is it wise?
Just find your laugh between the sighs.

Why do socks vanish in the wash?
Is there a sock thief, oh dear gosh?
Clothes take a trip while we stay still,
Is this just life or a wild thrill?

When do we truly start to find,
The secret jokes of the universe kind?
The coffee spills and broken toys,
Make room for chuckles and silly joys.

So raise a glass to this odd ride,
With giggles waiting just inside.
Beneath the craziness, a hoot,
Find joy in chaos, it's a hoot!

Enigmas Beneath the Surface

Why does cereal get soggy too fast?
Is breakfast a race that we just cannot last?
The toast burns while we play the fool,
Searching for meaning in a bowl of drool.

Maps show paths that make no sense,
We wander blindly; it's quite intense.
The compass spins while we ask with glee,
Is north really where we want to be?

What's the deal with all the hair?
It grows and grows, with no care to spare.
Do we need a cut or a wild style?
The barber's chair can make us smile.

So let's toast to these quizzical days,
Where answers hide in comical ways.
With every question, laughter swells,
In this grand riddle, our humor dwells!

Labyrinths of Existence

Is it just me, or has time gone awry?
Monday feels like Friday, oh my!
Clocks spin like tops, what's the score?
A week in a day, who could ask for more?

The cat seems wise, with secrets untold,
While we chase after dreams, brave and bold.
It's a jungle gym when looking for truth,
But laughter is easy; it's the fountain of youth.

Why do we worry about silly things?
Like whether a new pair of shoes sings?
In the game of life, we all play our part,
With giggles and snickers springing from the heart.

So dance through this maze with a wink and a grin,
For every twist and turn, a joke to spin.
In the madness, remember this way:
The fun is the answer, come what may!

The Puzzle of Our Days

Why do keys hide when you're in a rush?
It's a game they play, what a silly hush!
Every drawer hides a secret or two,
As we navigate chaos, it's all brand new.

Shuffling papers in a frantic quest,
Finding old notes with a pop quiz zest.
Who wrote this doodle? You'll never know,
In the mess of our minds, creativity flows.

Why does ice cream melt on a sunny day?
It's a treat that plays, come out to play!
With each cone drop, we laugh through bites,
Chasing sweetness 'neath the sunny lights.

Let's gather these pieces, have some fun,
Make sense of the chaos when day is done.
In this puzzle, with smiles to fill,
Find joy in the madness, it's a thrill!

Fog of Choices

In the morning haze, I choose my socks,
One pair's polka dots, the other like clocks.
Shall I eat toast, or maybe a cake?
Decisions so tricky, my brains start to ache.

Should I go left or right at the park?
A squirrel gives chase, my mind's in the dark.
The path looks too rocky, the grass is too tall,
I sit down to ponder, then tumble and fall!

A friend calls me up, says 'Why so perplexed?'
I chuckle and say, 'Hey, who needs context?'
With sheer absurdity, I'm living each day,
Wading through choices like ducks in a fray.

So here's my anthem, with laughter I sing,
Decisions so silly, oh what joy they bring!
I'll dance through the chaos, embrace the unknown,
For in this fog of choices, I'm never alone!

Reflections in the Abyss

Staring down deep in the bathroom mirror,
Who stares back at me? The image gets clearer.
With toothpaste on shirt, and hair like a mop,
I ponder my secrets, oh please, just stop!

The abyss of my thoughts is a funny old place,
Where socks go to vanish, and dreams lose their face.
I wink at my twin, who quirks just the same,
But alas, it's just me, playing a strange game.

What wisdom is hiding, behind all the grime?
Maybe the secret lies somewhere in rhyme.
With giggles I scribble my nonsense for fun,
In this reflection, I see every pun.

So should I retreat from this curious sight?
Or embrace my odd self and dance through the night?
The abyss may be deep, but I've got my flair,
Tickling the soul like a soft autumn air!

The Spiral of Understanding

Round and round in a merry-go-round,
Understanding grows, but it's lost and found.
What's up is down, and left has gone right,
I'm dizzy from thoughts, but oh what a sight!

I scribble my theories on napkins and walls,
Each idea like gum, on my shoe it just stalls.
I set out to ponder, then end up in jest,
With friends laughing hard, who needs all the rest?

A circle of mind-benders, giggling away,
Chasing the answers that lead us astray.
But what if the journey is where it's at?
Perhaps I'm a riddle, or just a friendly cat!

As I spiral and twirl through this puzzling jest,
I find all my moments are simply the best.
So let's spin together, in this wacky dance,
For it's in the confusion, we find our romance!

Notes from an Infinite Scroll

Endless the scrolling, my thumb feels a strain,
What was I seeking? Ah, what's on the train?
A cat in a hat, then a dog with a pie,
My scrolling adventures could surely make one cry!

From memes about coffee to tips on a diet,
Every click pulls me deeper, I can't help but buy it.
With laughter as currency, joy's free to share,
I'll forge my own path, without a care.

Notifications ping, 'You've missed out on fun!'
But what is 'fun' when all's said and done?
Is it chasing my dog, or a prank on a mate?
Or laughing through posts that confuse and create?

So here's to the scroll, with its comedy might,
It teaches that laughter is always in sight.
Though questions keep coming and answers may stall,
Let's laugh at the scroll and just have a ball!

Moments in a Tempest

In a storm of socks and shoes,
I dance through puddles, sing the blues.
Gusts of laughter whip me around,
While thunder claps, I might fall down.

A parrot squawks in a top hat,
He claims to solve this puzzle flat.
I ask him, 'What's my next big move?'
He just laughs, then starts to groove.

Rain pours like thoughts out of my head,
Each drop a clue I had misread.
I balance on a wobbly log,
A riddle wrapped in a friendly dog.

But as the winds begin to clear,
The answers disappear, oh dear!
I chuckle at this slippery game,
For questions sprout like weeds, not fame.

The Mirror of Illusions

I glance in mirrors, what do I see?
A doppelgänger grinning at me.
With googly eyes and a silly grin,
He whispers secrets of where to begin.

He points to paths with chocolate trees,
And dancing stars that spin with ease.
I ask, 'Is this all a big charade?'
He just chuckles, 'Life's a masquerade.'

Reflections twist like spaghetti strands,
Each one takes me to strange new lands.
A rabbit hops in with a light-up hat,
He says, 'Let's find where the answers sat!'

But as we peek through each silly pane,
The truths dissolve like sugar in rain.
In joy I ponder this crazy spree,
With mirrors tricking both you and me.

Threads of Mystery

In the loom of time, threads intertwine,
Some fray while others shine just fine.
Knots of laughter, tangles of tears,
A tapestry woven by silly fears.

I pull on a string, it leads to a cow,
Mooing loudly, 'What's your why, now?'
I scratch my head, he just chews grass,
In this tangled world, how time does pass!

A cat on a rug gives me a look,
Turns her back, as if reading a book.
'Hey! No spoilers!' I call with a grin,
But she just yawns, 'Let the fun begin!'

So I gather my threads, both bright and dim,
Each twist and turn, a chance to swim.
In knots we find the laughter so true,
Every jumbled path leads us to you.

Chasing Fleeting Answers

I chased a shadow down the lane,
It giggled softly, 'Catch me in vain!'
With a hop and a skip, I spun for joy,
But it zipped off like a cheeky toy.

A butterfly flutters with a wink,
Holding secrets, or so I think.
I chase it through flowers, bright and grand,
But it giggles, saying, 'Take my hand!'

Through fields of daisies, up hills so steep,
Where answers play hide-and-seek, not sleep.
I trip over riddles, tumble and roll,
In this mad dash, I find my soul.

So here I stand, no answers to find,
Just funny moments that twist in my mind.
With a wry smile, I let out a laugh,
For the chase is the riddle—what a daft path!

The Symphony of Uncertainty

In the orchestra of chance, we play,
A clarinet's squeak leads the fray.
With trumpets blaring, we skip and slide,
Dancing to rhythms we cannot decide.

The baton waves like a wild storm,
Who knows if this note will keep warm?
As cellos grumble with a witty sigh,
We trip on the beat, oh my, oh my!

A tambourine's jingle makes us laugh,
Not sure if it's fate or a gaffe.
Every movement's a joke that we tell,
In this grand symphony, we juggle quite well.

So raise a glass to the baffling show,
In the concert of chaos, let laughter flow.
With every sour note, we cheer with delight,
For dancing on tunes is our favorite sight.

Shadows in the Light

In a world where shadows wink and grin,
We chase them down with a goofy spin.
They flicker and tease, but what do they say?
Are they hints at the games we all play?

The sun's bright smile can't hide the jest,
Making silhouettes dance in weirdness blessed.
A shadow trips on its own two toes,
While we crack up at the silliness that grows.

With every flicker, a punchline appears,
We giggle at phantoms that hide our fears.
In laughter's embrace, the shadows conspire,
As we stumble together, our joy won't tire.

So come take a dance with the light and dark,
Where shadows fly past with a flick and a spark.
In this whimsical waltz, we find our delight,
For the world's a stage, let's dance through the night.

Fragile Threads of Fate

With threads so thin, we weave our tale,
Like spaghetti tangled—oh what a trail!
A knot in the yarn gives rise to a cheer,
Oh look! It's a hat—or just more junk near!

Each stitch a giggle, each loop a woe,
In this tapestry, we're set to go.
Our fabric of fortune, both silly and bright,
Is patched together with laughter and light.

Pull one thread, and the whole thing unspools,
Creating a spectacle of jumbled jewels.
With a wink at the chaos, we smile and say,
Where would we be without yesterday?

So let's thread together this whimsical fate,
With needles of humor, we can create.
In the loom of absurdity, we find our place,
For in every misstep, there's joy to embrace.

The Clockwork of Dreams

Tick-tock goes the dream machine,
With cogs of whimsy, it's quite the scene.
A gear might squeak, but we won't frown,
In this madcap world, we wear the crown.

Each hour spins tales so wacky and wild,
Like a kid with a prank, or a playful child.
The minute hand dances with glee so bright,
As we chase after dreams that take flight.

Our watches, they giggle with each little tick,
And laughter erupts with a comical trick.
When the seconds run fast, we climb on board,
Riding the whirlwind—we just can't be bored.

So let the clock strike with silly finesse,
In this carnival of time, we are blessed.
For every tick leads us back to our scheme,
In the clockwork of dreams, we find our gleam.

The Quest for Clarity

Wandering through fog and haze,
Seeking sense in silly ways,
Knocking on the doors of fate,
Who knew joy could be so great?

Questions tumble, answers prance,
Dancing in a wobbly dance,
Cobbled paths and tricky signs,
Laughter's found in twisted lines.

The map's a puzzle, lost and found,
Where reason flies and thoughts rebound,
A treasure hunt for wit and cheer,
Let's embrace the goofy sphere!

So grab your coat, your quirky hat,
We'll figure this out, or maybe not!
In a world where nonsense rules,
Together we'll unearth the jewels!

Misty Trails and Tangled Roots

Through the mist, the path goes twirling,
Around the bend, the gnomes are curling,
With roots that trip and rocks that tease,
I stumble forward, all with ease.

The trees are whispering, can you tell?
They've secrets wrapped in leafy spell,
Yet every step, a laugh ensues,
How'd I end up wearing these shoes?

Up ahead, the sky is blue,
But clouds keep laughing, what do they do?
Navigating through this jolly jest,
Finding my way, I'll do my best.

So raise a cheer for twisted trails,
With giggles echoing sweet as tales,
The journey's fun, though steps may fail,
In tangled roots, we'll always prevail!

Dreams Beneath the Surface

Beneath the layers of silly dreams,
Where nothing's quite as it seems,
Doodles dance and hiccups hum,
In a world where giggles come.

A swimming pool of wobbly thoughts,
Filled with fish that tie their knots,
I dive in deep with flair and grace,
But often come up with a pie on my face!

Flip-flops on the ocean floor,
Jellyfish and pizza galore,
Each bubble pops with a funny squeak,
In the dreams where laughter speaks.

So let's explore this zany sea,
With unexpected joy, wild and free,
The surface may be still and flat,
But underneath, it's a spontaneous spat!

The Scribe of Shadows

In shadows long, a scribe does weave,
Tales of whimsy that make you believe,
With every draft, the quill does jig,
Writing nonsense, both big and small pig!

Inking pranks with a sly little grin,
Stories of owls who lost their skin,
Mice in hats, plotting delight,
With giggles lurking just out of sight.

The parchment laughs, it bends and folds,
With bits of joy that never gets old,
A circle of chortles, a fountain of glee,
Creating chaos, oh woe is me!

So join the scribe with a pen in your hand,
Crafting humor in this wonderland,
For in each shadow lies a jest,
A world of laughter, we are truly blessed!

The Dance of the Unknown

In socks that don't quite match, we twirl,
Chasing the cat in a crazy whirl.
With breakfast cereal stuck in my hair,
I ponder the meaning—if only I dare.

The clock ticks backward as I make my toast,
Dreaming of pancakes, I lose my post.
The fridge hums secrets, it's keeping it tight,
I ask it questions as it beams with delight.

Step right up, here's the clown of the day,
Juggling my worries, watch them all sway.
With each goofy tumble and banana peel slip,
I laugh through the chaos—oh, what a trip!

In slippers and jammies, I take center stage,
I'm the star of this conundrum-filled page.
So here's to the twists, come join in the fun,
With every misstep, our laughter's begun.

Fragments of a Fading Horizon

In dreams that scatter like leaves in the breeze,
I try to catch answers, but they slip with ease.
The sun paints my breakfast a glorious gold,
Yet toast on my shirt is a sight to behold.

A riddle in shadows, the morning's delight,
The dog's stolen socks, what a whimsical sight!
As clouds shape a dragon, my worries take flight,
Laughing at questions that fade with the night.

The horizon blinks twice, then it winks at me,
With laughter akin to a wobbly bee.
I glance at my planner, it points to a chore,
But here in my heart, I wish to explore.

So I'll chase down the stars while I drink my tea,
Embracing the twists that make me feel free.
For fragments are magic, they shimmer and glow,
In this funny game, I'm ready to flow.

No Answers Under the Stars

Beneath the vast galaxy, I sit with a sigh,
The universe snickers, a twinkle nearby.
A cookie crumbles as I ponder the sky,
Are we just faint echoes, or do we still try?

The questions float freely, like dandelion fluff,
The answers play hide-and-seek, oh so tough!
With every wish launched, I giggle and wait,
For the cosmos to wink, like a date gone quite late.

My telescope's broken, it squints at the moon,
Yet here I am dreaming, I'll figure it soon.
Between the big dipper and my chocolate mess,
It's all so absurd, I just have to confess.

So here's to the mysteries that twirl in the dark,
To laughter and wonder with each silly spark.
Let's dance with confusion, we won't let it mar,
Under the night sky, we'll chase down a star.

The Maze of Daily Threads

In a labyrinth woven with morning mistakes,
I thread through a maze of mismatched pancakes.
The coffee pot whistles, it's cursed, I declare,
As I trip on my shoelace, a wild morning affair.

Dishes are lurking, they whisper my name,
"Join us for chaos, we're stirring up fame!"
I laugh with the fridge, it's a partner in crime,
Together we plot for a nonsense-filled time.

The calendar's crowded, oh what a sad tale,
With meetings and errands, I'm destined to fail.
Yet in all the mayhem, a bright spark of cheer,
As I wade through the chaos, I hold it all dear.

So let's stitch together this patchwork of days,
With humor and giggles, where chaos displays.
In the maze that we wander, we'll take one more thread,
For in joyful confusion, that's where dreams are fed.

Reflections of an Untold Journey

In a world of zig and zag,
I found a map that had no flag.
My compass spun, oh what a prank,
Do I stand tall, or walk the plank?

With socks that clash and shoes unmatched,
I sailed on puddles, perfectly patched.
The sun was late, the moon said hi,
Clouds giggled softly as they floated by.

Each step I took was a dance of chance,
With every stumble, I found romance.
The road ahead was wrapped in cheer,
Who knew adventure took a beer?

So here I sit, with tales to spin,
A jester's hat upon my chin.
My journey's tale is quite absurd,
Exciting whispers, never heard.

Threads of Curiosity

I pulled a thread, and out it came,
A snazzy sock, but where's the fame?
My cat wore it like a crown,
A furry prince, who'd never frown.

With every tug, a riddle formed,
A broccoli in a pumpkin, normed.
Should I bake a cake or spin a yarn?
This curious thread would lead to a barn.

Peeking through answers wrapped in fluff,
I questioned loudly, 'Is this enough?'
A labyrinth of questions flew,
Yet "why" was answered with "ask the shoe!"

A tangle here, a twisty knot,
In threads we weave, we find a lot.
So laugh with me, let's dance along,
In this ridiculous thread, we belong.

The Labyrinth of Dreams

Oh dreams, they waltz with twisty fate,
I chased a dragon, but was late to date.
With jellybeans for shoes, I flew,
What's that sound? Oh, it's just my shoe!

A map made of marshmallows and cheese,
I tripped on unicorns, if you please.
Each corner turned, a chuckle bloomed,
What's my mission? To eat my broom!

In this maze where giggles reign,
I met a snail who spoke in rain.
His wisdom wrapped in giggles tight,
"Tomorrow's breakfast is pizza night!"

So join the fun in this dreamy spread,
Where every turn's a feathered bed.
We'll giggle and sigh, let worries melt,
In this labyrinth where laughter's felt.

Footprints in the Mist

I wandered through a foggy street,
With shoes so squeaky, what a feat!
Each footprint left a puddle's mark,
Waddling onward, I missed the park.

A chicken crossed just to ask,
"If life is a joke, should I wear a mask?"
I chuckled back, then jumped a ditch,
Oh what a glorious, goofy glitch!

With every step, a giggly splash,
The mist grew thick, my thoughts a mash.
What if the clouds are thinking too?
"Who let that gopher drink the glue?"

As laughter echoed through the haze,
I danced with shadows in a daze.
Footprints in mist, a funny twist,
In every wanderer, a giggle's fist.

Twists in the Path

With every step, I trip and slip,
The road is wide, but I'm a little hip.
When I turn left, I find a right,
A map is just a jester's delight.

Potholes gang up, like pals in fun,
I dodge, I weave, on the run, run, run!
A squirrel laughs as I make a dash,
Oh, the paths we take for a simple snack!

The daisies dance in corners dim,
As I ponder why the sky is grim.
Do I take a bus, or just my heart,
To chase a dream that's not so smart?

Yet each wrong turn is a story bold,
A chapter where the laughs unfold.
With every twist and silly bend,
It seems the path does not quite end!

Whispers of Tomorrow's Dawn

Chasing shadows of the upcoming night,
The dawn plays tricks, oh what a sight!
Coffee spills as I dance with glee,
As whispers of dreams beg, 'Come to me!'

The rooster crows like a rockstar's tune,
While I can't find my left shoe at noon.
Tomorrow laughs with a winking eye,
"Who needs plans? Just give it a try!"

Dancing with hopes on a shaky floor,
As the clock ticks—could I ask for more?
Each tick and tock, a riddle to crack,
Tomorrow says, "Don't look back!"

With a skip and a hop, I jest and play,
In the game of now, we find our way.
Who needs maps when the sun's our guide?
Tomorrow smiles wide, filled with pride!

Threads of The Unraveled

Tangled yarns of brightly spun,
Knitting thoughts, oh what fun!
Each stitch a giggle, each knot a tease,
As I unravel dreams with ease.

Sock puppets dance with socks on their heads,
While I chase the cat, who leaps from beds.
"Why don't you knit me a clever hat?"
Says my spirit, while I sit flat!

The sweater once grand is a patchwork mess,
A puzzle of colors, oh what a stress!
Yet in every fray, there's laughter so bright,
Threads of confusion weave joy in the light.

In this quirky quilt of thoughts and dreams,
I find my peace in tangled seams.
With scissors and smiles, I carve my way,
In the threads of today, I choose to play!

Echoes in the Mind's Maze

Wandering through my mind so vast,
Thoughts echo like shadows cast.
Each corner hides a joke or two,
As I chase after my own "Who knew?"

The walls giggle with secrets well-kept,
While I search for dreams that are adept.
A maze of giggles, a loop-de-loop,
I tumble along, doing the loop.

"Left or right?" I ask aloud,
The silence chuckles, feeling proud.
Am I lost or on a spree?
The echoes reply, "Just be free!"

In this bright swirl of whims and fancies,
I dance with hopes and silly chances.
Every twist in the mind's grand parade,
Reveals the fun in the charade!

The Carnival of Choices

In the circus of options, we spin and we twirl,
Cotton candy decisions, flags all unfurl.
Do we ride the Ferris wheel, or eat a hot dog?
With each twist and turn, we feel like a frog.

Should I dance with a clown, or juggle some pies?
The noisemakers laugh as I squint at the skies.
Prancing through popcorn, oh where is the end?
With every misstep, I trip on a friend.

Round and round we go, a merry-go-fun,
Chasing the echoes of laughter, we run.
Is it a game or a trick of the light?
Guess I'll find out just before my next bite.

So choose and confuse, with glee in our eyes,
The choices keep coming, oh what a surprise!
In the carnival's grasp, I'll fumble and play,
For joy's the best riddle, at least for today.

Veils of Time

Tick-tock sings the clock, with secrets to share,
Wrapped up in moments, that vanish in air.
I blink and I'm older, what happened to youth?
Time plays hide and seek, while I chase the truth.

A time-traveling snail with a monocle ties,
Fumbles and tumbles, then laughs with wise sighs.
Each second a puzzle, a riddle divine,
Crawling to now, should I drink or just dine?

With hats made of minutes and shoes made of hours,
I waltz through the ages, on whimsical towers.
The past holds a mirror that's cracked down the side,
What's lost is just laughter, where time can't abide.

So I tiptoe and giggle, through shadows they cast,
In veils of the present, and echoes of past.
Life's just a carnival of seconds to seize,
Winding through mazes of joy and of tease.

The Book of Unwritten Pages

Here lies a tome of unwritten delight,
Pages that tease me, but just out of sight.
Inkwells of chuckles and pencils of glee,
What stories await on the next empty spree?

I scribble my dreams with a featherlight hand,
Each line is a quirk, a zany chant planned.
What if I tumble, or leap with a sprain?
Maybe the chaos will give me a gain.

The characters giggle, they prance and they play,
With twists that could topple a logical sway.
A plot twist with sprinkles, a twist with a frown,
I'll pen this tale upside down and 'round.

The book has no ending; it teems with surprise,
Each sentence a kaleidoscope of the wise.
So grab your own quill, and dance with your words,
In this book of the wacky, let your heart be heard!

Paths Undefined

In a forest of choices, paths twist like a vine,
Should I go left or right? Or sip some fine wine?
Each step is a giggle, a hop or a jump,
I'm lost in the shuffle like an optimistic lump.

The signs spin in circles, they chuckle and tease,
"Go here, go there! Or go talk to the bees!"
With every wrong turn, the perplexed feel I gain,
Dancing with shadows, I'll just entertain.

A jellybean road with flavors so bright,
I savor the journeys through morning and night.
Each corner I crest, a new riddle appears,
Should I rumble with trolls or just pet the dears?

With mischief pure magic, and laughter my guide,
I cherish the moments where whimsy abides.
For paths undefined lead to treasures untold,
And the wandering heart forever feels bold.

Threads of Mystery We Weave

In the cupboard of dreams, socks play hide and seek,
While spoons conspire in a pot, oh so meek.
The cat plots a scheme with a sock on its head,
As the toaster pops toast, 'I swear, I'm well-bred!'

Behind each closed door, secrets unfold,
A dance of confusion, both funny and bold.
The fridge hums a tune, while milk starts to pout,
In this tangled-up world, there's always a clout.

With every new dawn, questions arise,
Why does the toast jump, causing such surprise?
A puzzle of laughter, a whirlwind of jest,
In this curious game, we all are a guest.

As we spin through the threads, each day a new thread,
With laughter and joy, our worries we shed.
So bring on the riddles, let's twist and let's twine,
In this madcap adventure, everything's fine!

Whispers of Uncertainty

A pebble in shoes, oh what a strange game,
With every step forward, it whispers my name.
The squirrels in the park chuckle, 'What's that noise?'
As I dance with grievances, forgetting my poise.

Balloons float by, they're mocking my plans,
One popped with a laugh, 'You've got no chance, man!'
The sky drizzles rain, yet sunshine peeks sly—
Who knew weather had such a sense of dry?

In the fridge, a yogurt, its date is a blur,
Still I give it a whirl, could it be a cur?
Every corner I turn, mysteries bloom,
As socks start their tango, in a comical room.

Oh, the joy of not knowing, the giggles it brings,
Like an owl in a tux, doing sensible things.
With every odd moment, uncertainty's flair,
In this riddle of puzzlement, we lighten the air!

The Dance of Shadows and Light

Under the glow of a kitchen light,
A shadow does salsa, what a curious sight!
With a spoon and a plate, they twirl and they sway,
While I stand, bemused, dreaming of ballet.

The clock chimes as though it's singing a song,
While the dust bunnies plot right where they belong.
They hold their grand ball, with slippers of fluff,
In this silly soiree, have I had enough?

Jellybeans roll over, all colors collide,
In this banquet of chaos, we take quite a ride.
The dog takes a leap, thinking it's all for show,
'Was I invited?' he wags, putting on a glow.

In each twist of existence, humor we find,
The shadows have secrets, but aren't very kind.
So let's join their dance, and smile through the night,
For the moon's just a spotlight, shining so bright!

Echoes of the Unseen

Whispers of echoes bounce off the walls,
A sock's solitary journey, while laughter enthralls.
The fridge hums its tune, while we seek the remote,
"What's the secret?" I ponder, in my cozy boat.

Invisible friends are having a feast,
While I search for my keys, it's a never-ending beast.
The carpet giggles, as my shoes start to trip,
Join in the riddle, let's take a wild dip.

Toasters and teapots join hands for a chat,
While the rug rolls its eyes, 'What's up with that?'
The curtains are swaying, keeping up their charade,
In this world of unseen, a great masquerade.

Every twist and turn brings a chuckle or two,
With the hiccups of fate, we all make do.
So raise up your glasses to humor and jest,
In this baffling riddle, we're all truly blessed!

Puzzles in the Silence

In quiet rooms where shadows dance,
A sock will vanish, take a chance.
The coffee pot is full of dreams,
Yet spills its secrets, or so it seems.

When questions linger, no replies,
The cat, it thinks, is very wise.
With a twitch of tail and a sly glance,
It hides the truth behind a prance.

In whispers soft, the answer's near,
But laugh too loud, and it disappears.
A puzzle wrapped in a riddle's song,
Just when you're right, you find you're wrong.

In silence deep, the answers bloom,
Yet stampede in and clear the room.
So here we sit, puzzled and proud,
Enjoying silence, soft and loud.

Fleeting Whispers of Truth

Truth tickles softly, like a sneeze,
Just when you grasp, it dances, flees.
A spoon tries to stir what's set in stone,
While the wise old owl just hoots alone.

Questions flutter, like butter on toast,
Each one begs, "Am I the most?"
The clock chimes funny, with a silly face,
And time itself begins to race.

In the garden grows a bizarre fruit,
So sweet, yet there's no one to salute.
Chasing shadows, we play charades,
While echoes of truth just masquerade.

So giggle, wobble, and skip with glee,
For wisdom's just a joke, you see.
Catch the whispers, hold them tight,
But wear a grin: it's silly, right?

The Canvas of Dualities

Brush strokes of joy, splatters of dread,
Painted with laughter, it's all in your head.
Life's a canvas, both bright and dark,
With each little quirk, it leaves a mark.

A jester's hat upon a sage,
Wisdom wrapped in a showy page.
Flip the palette, mix up the hues,
In every choice, there's always clues.

A paradox strides with oversized shoes,
Tipping the scales, it laughs, it snooze.
Blindly we laugh at the cosmic jest,
For in these colors, we find our quest.

So paint your dreams with a light-hearted hand,
In this wacky world, we all must stand.
Embrace the mess, the giggles, the swings,
For every riddle, a chuckle it brings.

Conundrums at Dawn

In morning light, the puzzles play,
As coffee brews to greet the day.
The sun peeks out with a cheeky grin,
And questions dance, where to begin?

Clocks tick forward, then jump right back,
A calendar prank, that's just the knack.
The toast pops up, a slice gone rogue,
It's not burnt bread, just a joke on vogue.

Birds chirp riddles in melodic tones,
While squirrels chuckle, stealing our phones.
With each new dawn, the puzzles renew,
Dancing lightheartedly, like morning dew.

So wake with laughter, greet the unknown,
Embrace the quirkiness you've outgrown.
For in each conundrum, there's joy to unfold,
A cheeky reminder; be funny, be bold!

The Complicated Simplicity of Being

Why do socks always go missing?
They must be off on a journey.
Chasing dreams in the washing machine,
Or plotting against our laundry spree.

A cat that ponders the meaning of life,
Sitting on the windowsill so proud.
Yet as a fly buzzes, it shifts its gaze,
Whiskers twitching, oh that's loud!

The toaster dialogues with bread so warm,
To crunch or not, that is the quest.
While coffee steams with existential dread,
And hangs with milk, like a well-dressed guest.

In this circus of trivial pursuits,
We dance 'round joy, spinning like tops.
With every misstep, we laugh and we cheer,
For this conundrum, it never stops.

Secrets Carved in Time

Tick-tock goes the vintage clock,
Whispers of secrets long since forgot.
A gnome in the garden keeps watch at night,
Juggling the stars, what a curious sight!

Grandpa's old stories stir laughter and tears,
Spiced with odd truths and whimsical fears.
He says time travel's a trip through the fridge,
Where ice cream can fix every heart's smidge.

The calendar fights with its own little fate,
Scribbling plans it can't help but negate.
An umbrella's a poet on rainy days,
Spinning verses in most peculiar ways.

Each moment a puzzle, each second a game,
Wrapped tightly in riddles, yet oddly the same.
With crumpets and tea, we toast to the stars,
In this whimsical journey, we'll all be memoirs.

The Mirror's Silent Inquiry

Stand before the mirror, what do you see?
A hairstyle that's fighting with gravity.
The reflection winks, could it be a prank?
Or maybe it knows more than I can thank?

Collecting dust like a sage on the shelf,
The bathroom witness of our true self.
It asks questions in silence, with wise, glassy eyes,
As we craft our excuses wrapped in sweet lies.

A toothbrush confessions spill early each morn,
Where grudges dissolve with minty adorn.
And loofahs are sages in a lathered debate,
On scrubbing away all the crumbs of our fate.

Yet every glimpse holds a giggle or sigh,
As we ponder our laundry in the mirror's reply.
In this comedy show of reflections we roam,
The mirror just smiles, saying, "Welcome home."

Fragments of the Unspeakable

Once I lost a sock in a puzzle of fate,
Now it dances with dust bunnies, isn't that great?
A mismatch turned legend, a tale to behold,
Of the sock that escaped, brave and bold.

Chickens in wisdom wear glasses to think,
While pondering stories over glasses of pink.
They'll cluck about mysteries of farmer and field,
These fragments of nonsense they joyfully wield.

A jellybean's journey from jar to my heart,
Each flavor a question, each chew an art.
The candy shop whispers sweet secrets of lore,
Where gums of the past lead you out the door.

In this world of oddities, let laughter reign,
For in every muddle, a treasure remains.
With giggles and grins, we chase the absurd,
In fragments of nonsense, true joy is stirred.

www.ingramcontent.com/pod-product-compliance
Lightning Source LLC
Chambersburg PA
CBHW051659160426
43209CB00004B/959